cocktails
by Sainsbury's

50 irresistible cocktails for every occasion

Creating the perfect cocktail is a bit like assembling the ultimate boy band. There has to be a striking look, a creative line-up and the ability to inspire a loyal fan base. When all the parts work in harmony, you've got yourself a hit.

Whether the cocktails you create are classic or flamboyant, the cool thing is that they can reflect your personality, mood or occasion. Cocktails are all about having fun and embracing a spirit of spontaneity and adventure. You can concoct them at home, dream them up on holiday and even take them to visit friends and family. You're free to select your favourite flavour to top the bill, whether it's fruity blackcurrant, floral elderflower or tropical coconut, and dream up a winning combination.

You can even hone and test your skills by competing with your chums to make the most delicious cocktails from the same set of ingredients. And how about experimenting with matching food and cocktails? You could create a cocktail for a special birthday, Christmas or anniversary as a gift with a tailored description. I once invented the 'Mr and Mrs Byrne' – a cocktail in two parts for my dear friends Sean and Cath to enjoy

on their wedding day, and for the rest of their lives. Think about the flavour you're aiming for – whether it's creamy, aromatic, spicy, salty, zingy or fruity – and build it accordingly. And while you're at it, why not invent a cocktail for yourself? The joy of cocktails is that everyone has the power to enjoy their own signature drink!

Cocktails, like pop bands, follow styles and trends, and are constantly being reinvented to bring something new and inspirational. My advice is to explore and, above all, enjoy yourself. Remember, you're in charge of the mixing desk. Welcome aboard!

Olly Smith
Wine & spirits expert

Contents

History of the cocktail ≡

A delicious story

A cocktail can be many things, tall or short, shaken or stirred. It can be sweet, sour, dramatic and delicious. The cocktail can be a drink of celebration or commiseration but, when made correctly, it's never boring. In fact, no other drink screams sophistication, glamour or fun quite like the cocktail. However, there can also be something mysterious about the cocktail – from the origin of the name to the creation of the very first drink.

What's in a name?

Cocktails as we know them today can be traced back to the early 19th century. Depending on who you believe, their creation is attributable to one of two men. The first involves Mexican Princess Xochitl, who enjoyed a drink or two. Legend has it she caught the eye of the King, who declared that her name be known by all in his kingdom. We assume drinks became known as xochitls, which probably became cocktails!

> **'It's been suggested the name stems from a feather garnish – a cock tail'**

The other surrounds Creole apothecary Antoine Amédée Peychaud, who worked in the French quarter of New Orleans. He was known to serve a strong mixed drink, made with aromatic spices and bitters, in a small egg-cup called a coquetier. Customers would enter his bar and ask for a coquetel which, due to problems with pronunciation, later became cocktail.

It has also been suggested that the name stems from a Colonial feather garnish, as mentioned in James Fenimore Cooper's novel *The Spy*. Fictional character Betty Flanagan was a tavern keeper, who served French soldiers a drink garnished with the tail feathers of a rooster – a cock tail.

Shake, rattle and roll

By 1850 the craze for cocktails was all the rage in America's happening cities – New Orleans, New York and San Francisco. New innovations from ice machines to fancy liqueurs helped transform ordinary drinks into works of art, as skilled barmen got creative with ingredients. One such man was Jerry Thomas, who is responsible for the flashy showman antics as demonstrated by bartenders across the world. In fact, Jerry changed the world when it came to mixing drinks for, in addition to his superb juggling skills, he also penned the world's very first cocktail book, *The Bartender's Guide: How to mix drinks*, first published in 1862.

Another notable bar star of this era was William T. 'Cocktail Bill' Boothby, who manned the bar at San Francisco's Palace Hotel and coined the term 'mixologist'. This was an exciting time for cocktails, and America set the bar – high.

Going underground

There's nothing like a ban to popularise a craze, and America's 'Noble Experiment', otherwise known as Prohibition (1920-1933), drove the drinking classes underground. Speakeasies popped up everywhere, serving cleverly disguised, extremely potent drinks, while tourists fled to

> **'The ban on alcohol triggered an exile of American bartenders'**

Cuba and discovered the fun to be had with rum. The ban on alcohol also triggered an exile of American bartenders, who crossed the Atlantic to mix up a storm in Europe's most exclusive establishments.

Bartender Harry McElhone shipped off and opened Harry's Bar in Paris, Frank Meier found himself at the Paris Ritz Bar, and Harry Craddock headed to the London Savoy's American Bar, which is just as popular today. The roaring 20s embraced the cocktail like a long-lost friend and it epitomised the carefree attitude of a people learning how to enjoy themselves.

Just when it looked like nothing could stand in its way, World War II hit and the cocktail fell out of favour. Life was very serious and cocktails were deemed frivolous. These intoxicating concoctions were all but forgotten until the 1980s, when a new craze for sweet, rainbow-coloured drinks swept the nation. Garishly topped with umbrellas and chunks of exotic fruit, these were the drinks of choice for young party revellers.

Sipping comfortably

Although we've moved on, cocktails are still very much in fashion. Timeless classics like the Martini sit happily alongside modern combinations on menus across the world. They have

> **'Topped with umbrellas and exotic fruit, these were the drinks of choice for young party revellers'**

universal appeal – whether you're in your thirties or your nineties, there's something for everyone.

This book is dedicated to the art of the cocktail and is filled with recipes for every occasion – so get stuck in and enjoy your cocktails responsibly!

Glassware

Your choice of glass is important, and it's not just about aesthetics. While glassware can make or break the look of your beautifully crafted cocktail, the real reason behind knowing your highballs from your tumblers is to maximise your drinking pleasure – the right quantity at the right temperature is what good mixology is all about.

The highball

A highball or tall glass is a tall tumbler that holds between 300 and 400ml. They are generally used for drinks that have a small amount of alcohol combined with a large proportion of mixer, such as a whisky & soda or gin & tonic. Tall glasses, with their smaller surface area, help to keep drinks carbonated and cooler for longer than wide-rimmed glasses. They are usually filled with ice - to maintain a cool temperature in your warm, cradling hands - but you can also try keeping your highballs in the fridge.

Ideal for:
• Gin & tonic
• Vodka & cola
• Long Island iced tea
• Bloody Mary
• Mojito
• Sex on the beach
• Pimm's
• Moscow mule
• Soft drinks

The tumbler

The 'tumbler', 'old-fashioned' or 'rocks' glass is a squat tumbler that holds between 200 and 300ml, similar in shape to a highball but shorter and wider. It is most often used for short, mixed drinks and anything like whisky over ice or 'on the rocks', hence the name. As these drinks are usually poured over ice,

the wider surface area that would otherwise allow your drink to warm up is not a problem.

Ideal for:
• Black and White Russian
• Mai tai
• Anything 'on the rocks'

The cocktail

The shape of this glass reminds us of the classic Martini. But watch out, as the conical shape makes it easy to spill - this is definitely not one for the dance floor. You should use this sexy stemware for neat drinks and other classic cocktails that measure anything from 100 to 250ml. The long stem lets you hold the glass without warming the drink, and the conical shape lends itself to garnishes and rims - such as the salt rim of the Margarita. You can also try chilling the glass in the fridge and mixing your drink with ice before pouring.

Ideal for:
• Martini
• Cosmopolitan
• Daiquiri
• Any chilled, neat drink to be lingered over

If you're in any doubt, the main consideration is to choose one that works with the volume of your drink: a measure of Martini will languish in a highball, and a shot of Long Island iced tea will not quench a thirst.

Equipment

Creating the perfect cocktail is not just about the ingredients ¬ just like cooking, having the right equipment for the job is key. A few basic items are all you need to create masterpieces like a professional. Keep it all to hand when you're entertaining – you don't want to be rummaging around the kitchen drawers halfway through creating your delicious concoctions!

Shaker

The barman's best friend, this is the most important tool in your cocktail cabinet and essential if you want to show off your cocktail-making skills. They have even become collectors' items. Early shakers were made of silver, but today most are made of plated metal or stainless steel. The Boston shaker used by professionals is a two-piece – a metal 'tin' and a mixing glass of roughly equal size. Ice and the cocktail ingredients are added to the mixing glass where quantities can be seen. The tin is then placed on top of the mixing glass. The bartender makes sure of a good seal before shaking the contents thoroughly. A three-piece shaker (pictured left) contains a metal tumbler, a small lid with a fitted strainer and a solid cap.

Strainer

Very useful to strain out ice, seeds and fruit pieces, a cocktail strainer acts like a sieve when transferring the mixed cocktail from the shaker to a glass. The Hawthorn strainer, pictured left, is a disc with a handle and two or more stabilising prongs. A metal spring fixed around the edge of the rim rolls inward to fit inside the tin. You'll need one of these if you use a two-piece shaker.

Muddler

The strangely named muddler is used for crushing fresh ingredients, such as soft fruits and herbs like mint, and to help release the flavour, juice or oils. You can buy metal and rubber (pictured left) or wooden versions. It's important for creating drinks such as the Mojito, where the flavour must be extracted from lime, sugar and mint.

Measures or jiggers

Ensure your cocktails are made to perfection with a jigger spirit measure. Two stainless steel measures in 25ml and 50ml are good starters. Glass measures with the same volumes are also available. Or try a two-spirit measure, which combines two sizes in one handy little unit (pictured left).

Other bits & pieces

- Blender – good for crushing ice and blending ingredients into purées.
- Bar spoon – long enough to reach the bottom of highball glasses. Also ideal for floating spirits and cream and creating layers.
- Bar knife – sharp enough to slice fruit for garnishes.
- Lemon and lime squeezer/juicer – makes life a lot easier when you need fresh juices.
- Citrus zester – great when you need zest or for making peel twists as garnishes.
- Ice tongs – a handy tool when making drinks for guests.
- Ice scoop – perfect for filling your shaker or glasses with ice.

Techniques

Technical terms explained

Reading a cocktail recipe can sometimes leave you wondering where on earth to start. Shake? Strain? Muddle? It can all sound a bit confusing and complicated, sending you running in the opposite direction to the nearest glass of beer or wine, but we promise it couldn't be easier! In fact, our handy rundown of the most useful techniques will show you just how simple it is to create delicious drinks. We'll explain all those strange-sounding terms, so the only thing getting into a muddle will be your muddler.

Shaking

This technique is used for drinks with heavy ingredients that need a more vigorous means of mixing and chilling. Whether you're using a two- or three-piece shaker, ensure you have one hand at each end, and shake vertically, allowing the ice and liquid to travel the full distance of the shaker. With a two-piece shaker, pour the ingredients into the glass part, then attach the tin over the top to create a vacuum. With a three-piece, just make sure the lid and cap are secure before you start shaking.

Straining

Straining is used to separate ice and small fragments of fruit from your drink.

Three-piece cocktail shakers have a strainer already built in. When you've finished shaking, just remove the top cap, check the lid is still secure, and pour the liquid directly into a glass.

If you're using a two-piece cocktail shaker, you will need a Hawthorn strainer (see below and page 13) to strain your drinks.

Hawthorn straining

When you've finished shaking, place the shaker on a surface with the tin at the bottom and the glass part at the top. Slap the glass part to break the vacuum (you may need to do this a few times before it releases) and make sure all the liquid pours into the tin. Place the Hawthorn strainer on top of the tin, with its spring resting snugly inside, then pour the liquid through the strainer into your glass. Hold the shaker and strainer firmly while straining to avoid any spillages!

Stirring

This method should be used in drinks that are made up solely of spirits (such as the Martini), or drinks with very light mixers. Stirring is a more gentle technique for mixing cocktails and is used to delicately combine the ingredients for the perfect amount of dilution.

Follow the recipe you are using as some will have exact steps – for example, stirring a certain number of times – and some will require gentle stirring. This is to ensure the ice does not melt too quickly, diluting the drink.

Layering

This technique requires a steady hand and it may take a bit of practice before you get it perfect! It's great for shots made up of different spirits, like the B52, or for adding cream to top alcoholic coffees and hot chocolates. Follow the exact recipe, as the order you are directed to layer the ingredients will usually be a key factor in whether it works or not.

Pour the liquid slowly and carefully over the back of a teaspoon directly into your drink

Muddling

Muddling is usually instructed when you need to release the flavour or aroma of a herb, or to extract the juices of a fruit, which will help to add flavour to your drink. There is a specific piece of equipment for this technique, the muddler (see left and page 13), but you could also use a bar spoon, or even the back of a kitchen spoon, if that's all you have.

To muddle, gently push the herbs or fruit down into the bottom of the glass.

Garnishing

There are loads of ideas for garnishes, so be creative! It's best to stick to fruits used within your cocktail, or to make sure the garnish will complement the flavour of your drink. Here are a few tips:

Wedges – great for adding a bit of extra juice to the drink.

Zest & twists – use a zester to add decorative zest (right). Use the pointed part on the side of a zester to create thin twists.

Wheels – cut a thin slice from the centre of the fruit, then cut from the centre of the slice to its peel. Hook onto the glass.

The classics

Mojito

This refreshing favourite combines sweet and sour notes, and the citrus and mint flavours perfectly complement the potent kick of rum

- 50ml Sainsbury's superior white rum
- 25ml lime juice, freshly squeezed, plus 1 wedge to garnish
- 15ml sugar cane syrup
- 10 mint leaves, plus 1 mint sprig to garnish
- ice cubes, crushed
- soda water, to top up

1 Pour the rum, lime juice and sugar cane syrup into a highball glass.

2 Take the mint leaves in one hand and clap your other hand onto them, then add to the glass.

3 Fill the glass with crushed ice then, using a spoon, pull the ingredients up from the bottom of the glass and stir until combined.

4 Top with soda and garnish with a lime wedge and a mint sprig.

Top tip...

Clapping the mint leaves between your hands (as directed in step 2) will release the essential oils, adding delicious flavour to the Mojito

Cosmopolitan

Popular in bars all around the world, this tasty number has a distinctive pink tint and is typically served in a classic cocktail glass

- 25ml Absolut Citron vodka
- 12.5ml Cointreau
- 12.5ml lime juice, freshly squeezed
- 25ml cranberry juice
- ice cubes
- orange peel, made into a twist to garnish

1 Pour all the ingredients into a cocktail shaker, fill with ice and shake hard.

2 Strain into a cocktail glass and garnish with an orange peel twist.

Vodka

Cointreau

Long Island iced tea

Developed during the Prohibition era, the name of this cocktail was chosen to mislead and disguise the potent ingredients within

- ice cubes
- 12.5ml basics vodka
- 12.5ml basics white rum
- 12.5ml basics gin
- 12.5ml tequila
- 12.5ml Cointreau
- 20ml lemon juice
- 12.5ml sugar cane syrup
- cola, to top up
- lemon wedge, to garnish

1 Fill a highball glass with ice and add all the ingredients, except the cola.

2 Stir gently, then drizzle the cola into the glass until it's full.

3 Garnish with a lemon wedge.

The basics

Use products from our basics range for cocktails made with lots of different spirits – they're great value

Vodka

White rum

Gin

Tequila

Cointreau

Martini

One of the world's best-known cocktails, the Martini is synonymous with style and class

- ice cubes
- 12.5ml Sainsbury's extra dry vermouth
- 75ml Sainsbury's London dry gin
- 1 olive, to garnish (plus 1-2 tablespoons brine from the olive jar if you like your Martini 'dirty')

For a dry Martini:

1 Fill a cocktail shaker with ice and add the vermouth. Stir 20 times, then strain out the vermouth and discard.

2 Add the gin, then stir gently.

3 Strain into a cocktail glass and garnish with an olive.

For a wet Martini:

1 Follow the steps above but do not strain and discard the vermouth.

For a 'dirty' Martini:

1 Follow the steps above for a dry or wet Martini, but add the brine from the olive jar.

Strewth, no vermouth?

Stirring vermouth with ice will give the ice an aromatic flavour. When you stir that ice with gin and strain into a glass, the flavour will remain, but as you've discarded the vermouth, none of its potency will transfer into your drink

Bloody Mary

This well-known ruby-red classic tastes good whatever the season. Add or subtract spice to suit your taste buds

- 50ml vodka
- 12.5ml lemon juice, freshly squeezed
- 4 dashes Worcestershire sauce
- 2 dashes Tabasco® sauce
- 2 pinches black pepper
- 2 pinches salt
- tomato juice, to top up
- ice cubes
- lemon wedge and celery stick, to garnish

1 Combine all the ingredients in a highball glass and fill with ice.

2 Stir gently, then garnish with a lemon wedge and a stick of celery.

Daiquiri

This delightful sweet and sour cocktail is the perfect balance of rum, sugar syrup and sharp citrus juice

- 50ml white rum
- 25ml lime juice, freshly squeezed
- 12.5ml sugar cane syrup
- ice cubes
- lime peel, made into a twist to garnish

1 Combine all the ingredients together in a cocktail shaker, fill with ice and shake hard.

2 Strain into a cocktail glass and garnish with a lime twist.

Strawberry daiquiri

A popular variation of this classic is a frozen strawberry daiquiri. Just place all the above ingredients in a blender, add a handful of hulled strawberries and whizz until the ice is crushed, then pour straight into a glass

The classics

Americano

An acquired taste, the bitter Campari and sweet vermouth balance nicely for lip-smacking flavours

- ice cubes
- 35ml Campari
- 35ml Sainsbury's vermouth rosso
- soda water, to top up
- lemon and orange peel, made into twists to garnish

1 Fill a tumbler with ice, pour in all the ingredients and stir gently.

2 Garnish with 1 lemon twist and 1 orange twist.

Did you know...

The Americano was Count Camillo Negroni's favourite drink, but one day he decided he'd like something stronger. He asked his bartender to swap the soda in the Americano for gin – this new drink became known as a Negroni. To make a Negroni, swap the soda water in the above recipe for 35ml gin

Campari

Sweet vermouth

Margarita

No one can agree exactly who invented the Margarita, but one thing is for sure, it's an incredibly delicious and stylish cocktail

- 35ml tequila
- 15ml Cointreau
- 25ml lime juice, freshly squeezed, plus 1 slice to garnish
- 12.5ml sugar cane syrup
- ice cubes
- slice of lime, cut to look like a wheel, to garnish

1 Combine all the ingredients in a cocktail shaker, fill with ice and shake hard.

2 Strain into a cocktail glass, then garnish with the lime wheel on the rim of the glass.

Sip with salt

If you like a salt rim on your Margarita, dip the rim of the cocktail glass in a little lime juice and roll in a plate of salt. If you're making Margaritas for friends and you're not sure they like a salt rim, just coat half the glass, then they can drink from whichever side they prefer

Moscow mule

This cocktail is so simple to make, but the taste is superb. It's a great drink to serve when unexpected guests pop round

- 50ml Taste the Difference Polish vodka
- 25ml lime juice, freshly squeezed, plus 1 wedge to garnish
- 1 dash Angostura® bitters
- ice cubes
- ginger beer, to top up

1 Pour the vodka, lime juice and bitters into a highball glass, stir gently and add some ice.

2 Top up with ginger beer and garnish with a lime wedge.

Did you know...

This cocktail was invented when John G. Martin (a spirits and food distributor) and John Morgan (a ginger beer producer) got together in a bar. Discussing their products, Martin wondered what his vodka would taste like with Morgan's ginger beer – the result was good. The drink has been refined, but the base of vodka and ginger beer remains

Mai tai

This powerful cocktail is fruity and fun – the tropical flavours will have you dreaming of sunny skies and sandy beaches

- 20ml Sainsbury's superior white rum
- 20ml Taste the Difference golden rum
- 20ml Cointreau
- 25ml lime juice, freshly squeezed, plus 1 wedge to garnish
- 10ml sugar cane syrup
- 5ml Taste the Difference almond extract
- ice cubes
- pineapple wedge, skin removed, plus 1 pineapple leaf, both to garnish (optional)
- 1 cocktail cherry, to garnish

1 Pour all the ingredients into a cocktail shaker, fill with ice and shake hard.

2 Crush some ice and add to a tumbler, then strain the liquid from the shaker into the glass.

3 Thread a pineapple wedge, lime wedge and cherry onto a cocktail stick, and balance over the glass. Place a leaf from the pineapple into the glass with a straw.

Did you know...

The most famous story behind the Mai tai is that of Victor J. Bergeron (aka Trader Vic). On serving the drink to some friends, one exclaimed 'Maita'i roa ae!' – literally 'very good', figuratively 'out of this world! The best!' – the Mai tai was born

White rum

Golden rum

Cointreau

Summer parties

Serves 4

Units: 1.3

Pimm's cocktail

Infused with aromatics, this gin-based drink is a summertime favourite – perfect for sharing

- ice cubes
- 200ml Pimm's No.1
- 800ml lemonade, to top up
- strawberries, hulled and halved
- apple, cored and sliced
- 1/2 cucumber, sliced
- mint leaves

1 Fill a jug with ice and add the Pimm's.

2 Top with lemonade and throw in some strawberries, apple, cucumber and mint leaves, then stir well.

Tickle your fancy

Don't just stick to the fruit we've suggested – anything goes, so get creative!

Brandy citrus squeeze

Combining refreshing citrus and smooth brandy, this drink is a sophisticated little delight

- 50ml brandy
- 100ml fresh orange juice
- squeeze of lemon juice
- ice cubes
- 2 orange slices, to garnish

1 Pour all the ingredients into a cocktail shaker, fill with ice and shake hard.

2 Fill 2 tumblers with ice cubes and strain the liquid into the glasses. Garnish with orange slices.

Dandy without brandy?

For a non-alcoholic summer refresher, omit the brandy and pour all the ingredients into a jug, then top up with lemonade or bitter lemon

Serves 1

Units: 0.9

Strawberry blush

Fizzy, fruity and a gorgeous pinky-red colour, this cocktail is bound to become a firm favourite

- handful of strawberries, hulled
- ice cubes
- 25ml vodka
- Sainsbury's cloudy lemonade, to top up
- mint sprigs, to garnish

1 In a blender, whizz the strawberries until you have a smooth consistency, then pour into a glass filled with ice.

2 Add the vodka and cloudy lemonade, then stir gently and garnish with mint sprigs.

Tropical paradise

More than simply rum and pineapple, this sunburst-coloured refresher includes a delicious hint of orange, mango and lime too

- 100g fresh pineapple, chopped, plus pineapple wedges to garnish
- ice cubes
- 100ml Taste the Difference golden rum
- 50ml Taste the Difference orange, mango & lime juice

1 Whizz the pineapple in a blender until puréed.

2 Fill a cocktail shaker with ice. Add the rum, puréed pineapple and orange, mango & lime juice, and shake well.

3 Fill 2 glasses with ice and strain in the liquid, then garnish with the pineapple wedges.

Mix it up

If fresh pineapple is unavailable, you can replace it with 100ml fresh pineapple juice. To turn it into a party punch, also add a sparkling mixer like soda

Sangria

Why not bring the holiday flavours of this popular Spanish drink home by making your own delicious sangria?

- 1 x 75cl bottle Sainsbury's House Torla Rioja
- 50ml vodka
- 1 orange, halved and sliced
- 1 lemon, sliced
- 1 peach, sliced
- 2 cinnamon sticks
- 500ml lemonade
- ice cubes, to serve

1 The night before you need it, pour the wine and vodka into a jug, then add the fruit and cinnamon and leave to steep overnight.

2 Stir gently, then top up with the lemonade and plenty of ice.

Summer parties

 Serves 4
Units: 1.4

Lime, lemon & ginger refresher

Packed with zesty flavour and especially good when it's getting hot, this ginger zinger is a drink that won't disappoint

- 6 lemons, 5 juiced and 1 sliced
- 6 limes, 5 juiced and 1 sliced
- 100ml sugar cane syrup
- 150ml vodka
- ice cubes
- 500ml ginger beer
- 250ml sparkling water

1 Mix the lemon and lime juice with the sugar cane syrup and vodka.

2 Fill a jug with ice and pour in the vodka mixture.

3 Add the sliced lemon and lime to the jug, then pour in the ginger beer and sparkling water, and stir.

Make it a mocktail

To turn this into an alcohol-free thirst quencher, leave out the vodka and add an extra 50ml ginger beer and 100ml sparkling water

Serves 1
Units: 1.8

Choco-coffee ice

A milkshake with va-va-voom, this creamy cocktail with an undercurrent of brandy and whisky is deliciously smooth

- 1 tablespoon instant coffee
- 3 tablespoons boiling water
- ice cubes
- 25ml basics brandy
- 50ml Irish cream liqueur
- 200ml full-fat milk
- 2–3 tablespoons single cream
- cocoa powder, to garnish

1 In a cocktail shaker, dissolve the coffee in the boiling water. Add a couple of ice cubes and allow the mixture to cool slightly, then add the brandy and Irish cream liqueur, and shake hard.

2 Fill a tall glass with ice, then pour over the coffee mixture. Add the milk, leaving an inch or so at the top for the cream, and stir.

3 Top with the cream and dust with cocoa powder.

Brandy

Irish cream
liqueur

Raspberry Prosecco cocktail

Fruity and gently sparkling, this cocktail is easy to put together at home and adds a touch of elegance to any drinks party

- punnet of fresh raspberries, reserving some to garnish
- 2 teaspoons caster sugar
- 1 x 75cl bottle Taste the Difference Prosecco Conegliano Superiore

1 Whizz the raspberries with the caster sugar in a blender until puréed.

2 Sieve to remove the seeds, then spoon into 6 flutes and top up with chilled Prosecco.

3 Stir gently, then garnish with a few fresh raspberries.

Blissful Bellini

Substitute the raspberries with 2 puréed peaches and you have a Bellini cocktail. Prosecco is the perfect base for this drink as it doesn't overpower the flavour of the fruit as Champagne can do

Orange passion

Brighten up your guests' day with this gorgeous blend of orange-flavoured liqueur, fresh orange and lemonade

- ½ x 2 litre bottle Sainsbury's cloudy lemonade
- 300ml Cointreau
- 2 oranges, sliced
- ice cubes
- seeds from 2 passionfruit, to garnish

1 Pour the lemonade and Cointreau into a large jug. Add the orange slices and stir well.

2 Pour into glasses filled with ice and garnish with passionfruit seeds.

Summer parties

Blackberry, lemon & gin fizz

This stunner of a cocktail blends juicy blackberries with gin for a truly mouthwatering tipple

- 5 blackberries, plus 1 extra to garnish
- ice cubes
- 25ml London dry gin
- lemonade, to top up
- lemon wedge, to garnish

1 In a highball glass, muddle the blackberries.

2 Fill the glass with ice and add the gin.

3 Top with the lemonade and garnish with a wedge of lemon.

In a muddle?

To 'muddle' the blackberries (see step 1), gently push them down into the bottom of the glass using the back of a spoon or a muddler (see page 13), until they resemble a purée

Retro favourites

Retro favourites

Tequila sunrise

The grenadine naturally settles below the orange juice in this drink giving a gorgeous sunrise effect

- ice cubes
- 45ml tequila
- orange juice, to top up
- 15ml grenadine
- orange slice, to garnish
- lime wedge, to garnish
- cocktail umbrella, to decorate

1 Fill a highball glass with ice, then add the tequila and orange juice.

2 Drizzle in the grenadine and garnish with an orange slice, a lime wedge and a cocktail umbrella.

Serves 1

Units: 1.2

Woo woo

One of the world's most recognised cocktails, this tipple is so good they named it twice

- ice cubes
- 25ml vodka
- 12.5ml peach schnapps
- cranberry juice, to top up
- lime wedge, to garnish

1 Fill a highball glass with ice.

2 Pour in the vodka and peach schnapps, then top up with cranberry juice.

3 Stir gently and garnish with a lime wedge.

Groovy garnish

Try carefully slicing the peel away from a lime wedge to about halfway up, then use the cut-away peel to hook the wedge onto the edge of the glass (see picture)

Vodka

Peach schnapps

Retro favourites

Snowball

This old favourite has a velvety texture and rich creaminess - it's high time we all rediscovered it!

- ice cubes
- 40ml Advocaat
- juice of 1 lime wedge
- lemonade, to top up
- orange slice, halved, to garnish

1 Fill a highball glass with ice.

2 Add all the ingredients to the glass, stir gently and garnish with the orange slice.

Retro favourites

Piña colada

Puerto Rico's official drink since 1978, this fruity, creamy concoction even has its own song

- ice cubes
- 40ml Malibu Caribbean rum
- 50ml pineapple juice
- 50ml full-fat milk
- pineapple wedges, to garnish (optional)

1 Fill a highball glass with ice.

2 Pour all the ingredients into the glass and stir gently, then garnish with 2 pineapple wedges.

Retro favourites

Harvey Wallbanger

Reported to have been invented in 1952 by three-time world champion mixologist Donato 'Duke' Anato, this is a fruity favourite

- ice cubes
- 45ml vodka
- 15ml Galliano
- 125ml orange juice
- orange slice, halved, to garnish

1 Pour all the ingredients into a shaker, fill with ice and shake hard. Fill a highball glass with ice.

2 Strain the liquid into the glass and garnish with the orange slice.

What's in a name?

Legend has it that this drink was named after a Manhattan Beach surfer who was a regular at Donato's bar in Hollywood in the early 1950s

Sex on the beach

Grab your sunglasses and a cocktail umbrella, whip up this drink and pretend it's summertime even when it's raining outside

- ice cubes
- 40ml vodka
- 20ml peach schnapps
- 50ml orange juice
- 50ml cranberry juice
- orange slice, to garnish
- cocktail umbrella, to decorate

1 Fill a highball glass with ice, then add the vodka, peach schnapps and orange juice.

2 Drizzle in the cranberry juice, then garnish with an orange slice and a cocktail umbrella.

Vodka

Peach schnapps

Retro favourites

White Russian

One of the first popular vodka-based drinks, this cocktail is a tasty after-dinner treat

- 50ml vodka
- 20ml Tia Maria
- ice cubes, crushed
- 35ml full-fat milk
- cocktail cherry, to garnish

1 Pour the vodka and Tia Maria into a tumbler and fill with crushed ice.

2 Add the milk, then stir gently and garnish with a cocktail cherry.

Swap shop

For a Black Russian, follow the steps above but don't add the milk or cherry

Vodka

Tia Maria

Blue lagoon

The original beach-holiday drink, this has a fantastic vibrant blue colour and equally fabulous taste

- ice cubes
- 35ml vodka
- 15ml blue curaçao
- lemonade, to top up
- lime wedge, to garnish

1 Fill a highball glass with ice.

2 Add all the ingredients to the glass, then stir gently and garnish with a lime wedge.

Serves 1

Units: 1.5

Retro favourites

Sea breeze

A well-known cocktail that appears in plenty of films and television shows, the bitter grapefruit balances nicely with fruity cranberry

- ice cubes
- 40ml vodka
- 40ml grapefruit juice
- cranberry juice, to top up
- lime slice, cut to look like a wheel, to garnish

1 Fill a glass with ice and add all the ingredients.

2 Stir gently and garnish with the lime wheel on the rim of the glass.

Make it a mocktail

This drink is equally as tasty without the vodka, and very refreshing

Serves 1
Units: 0.8

B52

It may take a few attempts to get this shot looking so neatly layered, but practice makes perfect!

- 10ml Tia Maria
- 10ml Taste the Difference Irish cream liqueur
- 10ml Grand Marnier

1 To get the layered effect, pour each spirit slowly and carefully in the order shown (left) over the back of a teaspoon, straight into a shot glass.

Retro favourites

Tia Maria

Irish cream
liqueur

Grand Marnier

Winter warmers

Winter warmers

Spiced brandy chai

This luscious blend of exotic spices, brandy and chocolate is too good to be kept to yourself!

- 400ml full-fat milk
- 6 cardamom pods, crushed
- 4 cinnamon sticks
- 4 cloves
- 100ml basics French brandy
- 20g dark chocolate, grated, plus extra to garnish

1 Put all the ingredients in a pan over a low heat and heat gently until warm.

2 Strain into 2 heatproof glasses and garnish with a little grated chocolate.

Winter warmers

Pack a tropical punch

Smooth Jamaican rum, with its touch of spice and hint of caramel flavour, is the base for this warming party punch

- 600ml pineapple juice
- 600ml orange juice
- 150ml Sainsbury's superior dark rum
- few dashes Angostura® bitters
- 2 limes, zest and juice
- 5 cardamom pods, crushed
- 3cm piece of fresh ginger, peeled and sliced
- 4 tablespoons light soft brown sugar
- 1 orange, thinly sliced

1 Pour the pineapple juice, orange juice, rum and bitters into a large saucepan. Add the remaining ingredients and stir over a low heat until the sugar has dissolved.

2 Bring to simmering point, then remove from the heat and ladle into 6 heatproof glasses.

The heat is on

When heating alcoholic drinks, do not allow the mixture to boil as this will burn off the alcohol

Hot spiced cider

Easy to make and delicious to drink – warm up any winter gathering with this tasty concoction

- 2 x 500ml bottles Taste the Difference vintage cider
- 30ml golden rum
- 6 cloves
- 1 apple, cored and sliced
- 6 cinnamon sticks

1 Place all the ingredients in a pan over a low heat and warm through.

2 Remove from the heat and pour into 6 heatproof glasses. Garnish each with a cinnamon stick from the pan.

Apple punch

For a non-alcoholic version, use a good-quality apple juice instead of cider and leave out the rum

Winter warmers

Serves 6
Units: 0.8

Nice 'n' spicy apple pie

A great drink to sip by the fire on a cold winter evening, once you've tried this easy recipe it's one you'll come back to

- 2 x 500ml bottles Taste the Difference Suffolk cyder
- 2 teaspoons brown sugar
- squeeze of lemon juice
- 6 cinnamon sticks
- red apple and lemon slices, to garnish

1 Gently simmer the Suffolk cyder, sugar, lemon juice and cinnamon sticks in a pan until warm.

2 Pour into 6 heatproof glasses, then garnish with the apple and lemon slices, along with the cinnamon sticks from the pan.

Serves 1

Units: 1.7

Winter warmers

Southern soother

Red wine pairs perfectly with Southern Comfort, a fruit, spice and whisky-flavoured liqueur, to make a deliciously smooth drink

- 25ml Southern Comfort
- 50ml red wine
- 25ml apple juice
- 1 small cinnamon stick
- 1 star anise, plus 1 extra to decorate
- 1–2 teaspoons caster sugar
- dash Angostura® bitters
- lemon slice, halved, to garnish

1 Place all the ingredients in a small pan. Heat slowly to a gentle simmer.

2 Pour into a heatproof glass and garnish with the star anise and lemon slice.

Easy Irish hot chocolate

If you love coffee with a bit of a kick, try this creamy hot chocolate version to keep the chills at bay

- 60ml Taste the Difference Irish cream liqueur
- 1 tablespoon cocoa powder
- 200ml coffee, prepared to your liking
- hot full-fat milk, whisked until frothy
- chocolate, shaped into curls using a peeler, to garnish

1 Pour the Irish cream liqueur into a small pan, then add the cocoa powder and heat until warm, stirring to make sure all the cocoa dissolves.

2 Stir in the brewed coffee, then pour into 2 heatproof glasses or mugs, leaving space at the top of each.

3 Spoon the frothy milk on top and garnish with chocolate curls.

Mulled red wine

With a hint of spice and sugar, and a delicate citrus tang, this tasty winter drink will help beat the next big freeze

- 150g light brown sugar
- 6 star anise
- 1 cinnamon stick
- 2 cloves
- zest and juice of 5 clementines
- 1 x 75cl bottle Sainsbury's House Merlot NV

1 In a pan, over a low heat, stir together the sugar, star anise, cinnamon stick, cloves and clementine zest and juice. Let the sugar dissolve in the juice, then turn up the heat and cook for another 5 minutes, until syrupy.

2 Stir in the red wine and heat for 5 minutes, making sure the mixture doesn't boil. Pour into 6 heatproof glasses and garnish with the star anise from the pan.

Mull it over

Use either a stainless steel, ceramic, heatproof glass or non-stick pan to mull the wine. The acids in the wine can react with aluminium and give it a metallic taste

Mulled white wine

Honey, ginger and vanilla are used to complement the flavours of white wine for a twist on the traditional that's just as delicious

- 150g runny honey
- 10g fresh ginger, peeled and finely grated
- zest and juice of 1 orange
- 3 cardamom pods, crushed
- 1 vanilla pod, cut in half lengthways
- 1 x 75cl bottle Sainsbury's House Chardonnay NV

1 Place the honey, ginger, orange zest and juice, cardamom pods and vanilla pod into a medium-sized pan. Heat over a low-to-medium heat for about 5 minutes, until syrupy, then pour in the wine.

2 Turn up the heat slightly and bring to the boil. When it reaches boiling point, take off the heat immediately and pour into 6 heatproof glasses.

On the go

The good thing about mulled wine is that you can keep adding to it – great if unexpected guests arrive. Keep it barely at simmering point but do not continue to boil or all the alcohol will evaporate

Hot toddy

There's nothing better than this traditional balance of spice, lemon, honey and whisky to beat the winter chill

- 150ml whisky
- 200ml water
- 1 tablespoon runny honey
- 1 lemon, zest and juice
- 2 cinnamon sticks, broken in half
- 8 cloves

1 Place all the ingredients in a small pan and stir over a low heat until just simmering.

2 Pour into 4 heatproof glasses and garnish with half a cinnamon stick from the pan to serve.

Toddy tips

You can replace the whisky in this recipe with rum if you like your cocktails a little sweeter, or brandy (or Cognac), which makes a very well-balanced hot toddy

Winter warmers

Traditional Irish coffee

A classic cocktail of coffee and Irish whiskey, topped with smooth, double cream - an indulgent treat

- 1 mug coffee, prepared to your liking, leaving space at the top of the mug
- dash Sainsbury's Irish whiskey
- 2 teaspoons sugar
- double cream, to top up

1 Stir the whiskey and sugar into your mug of coffee.

2 Pour the cream into the coffee slowly over the back of a spoon, so it sits on top.

Spirit of change

If you fancy a bit of a change, other spirits work equally well – try rum, brandy or Tia Maria to get you started

Festive flavour

Serves 12

Units: 1.6

Sparkly red wine punch

This delicious punch is perfect for parties – just place a ladle and some glasses next to the bowl and let your guests help themselves

- ice cubes
- 1 x 75cl bottle basics Spanish red wine
- 50ml basics French brandy
- 500ml orange juice
- 75cl sparkling white wine
- 2 apples, finely sliced
- 2 oranges, sliced
- pomegranate seeds, to garnish (optional)

1 Fill a large glass bowl with ice and add all the ingredients.

2 Stir well, then garnish with pomegranate seeds.

Back to basics

The great-value basics products in this recipe won't break the bank and are perfect for making flavour-filled punches

Red wine

Brandy

Sparkling wine

Serves 1

Units: 2

Candy cane cooler

This super-stylish cocktail is the ultimate festive treat. The cute little candy cane is a perfect finishing touch

- 50ml Taste the Difference Polish vodka

- 3 drops peppermint essence

- ice cubes

- lemonade, to top up

- small candy cane, to garnish

1 Pour the vodka into a cocktail shaker. Add the peppermint essence, fill with ice cubes and shake hard.

2 Strain into a cocktail glass and top up with lemonade.

3 Place the candy cane in the glass with the hook over the edge.

Quality taste

Our Taste the Difference vodka adds a sophisticated flavour to this tasty little number

Festive flavour

Elderflower Champagne

Why not make your Champagne even more special by adding a flavoursome twist and a touch of colour?

- 25ml Taste the Difference English elderflower cordial
- 1 glass Champagne, chilled
- pomegranate seeds, to garnish

1 Pour the cordial into a Champagne flute.

2 Top up with Champagne and garnish with pomegranate seeds.

Sparkling saving

If you've got a large number of guests or are saving your pennies for festive gifts, just swap the Champagne in this recipe for sparkling wine – it's just as tasty

Festive flavour

Serves 1
Units: 2.3

Velvet brandy

Warming brandy and moreish Irish cream liqueur are a match made in heaven in this beautiful drink

- 50ml brandy
- 30ml Taste the Difference Irish cream liqueur
- 30ml double cream
- ice cubes
- grated nutmeg, to serve

1 Mix together the brandy, Irish cream liqueur and double cream in a cocktail shaker, then fill with ice and shake well.

2 Strain into a cocktail glass and garnish with a little grated nutmeg.

Seasonal gin & ginger

Bitter gin and fiery ginger beer work in harmony to create a refreshing, spicy tipple – perfect for aficionados of the gin & tonic

- ice cubes
- 100ml basics gin
- 400ml ginger beer
- 4 limes, cut into wedges, to garnish
- 4 mint sprigs, to garnish

1 Fill 4 highball glasses with ice.

2 Pour in the gin and top with the ginger beer, then stir gently.

3 Garnish with the lime wedges and mint sprigs.

Serves 1

Units: 0.9

Santa's hat

This tasty work of art is simple to throw together and sure to impress with its Santa-themed creativity

- granulated sugar, to rim the glass
- ice cubes
- 25ml vodka
- 50ml cranberry juice
- 25ml orange juice
- small bunch of redcurrants, to garnish

1 Dip the rim of a cocktail glass into water, then into a plate of sugar to create the 'fluff' on Santa's hat.

2 Pour the vodka, cranberry juice and orange juice into a cocktail shaker, then fill with ice and shake hard.

3 Strain into the decorated glass and hook the redcurrants on the side.

Designated driver?

It's always a good idea to look after the designated drivers and non-drinkers at your festive parties. For a tasty, alcohol-free tipple, just remove the vodka from this recipe and add a little extra juice

Festive flavour

Mulled wine martini

Seasonal spices, enticing aromas and tangy fruit make this mulled wine with a difference taste as good as it looks

- ¼ teaspoon ground cinnamon
- 1 tablespoon golden caster sugar
- juice of 1 orange, freshly squeezed
- 200ml Taste the Difference mulled wine
- 30ml Sainsbury's vermouth rosso
- ice cubes
- 2 star anise, to garnish
- orange peel twists, to garnish

1 Mix the cinnamon with the sugar on a small plate. Dip the rims of 2 cocktail glasses in a little of the orange juice, then in the sugar, slowly turning so only the outer edge of the glasses are covered.

2 Add the mulled wine, vermouth and remaining orange juice to a cocktail shaker, fill with ice and shake hard.

3 Strain into the decorated glasses and garnish with the star anise and orange peel twists.

Festive flavour

Dom Pedro

This smooth and creamy cocktail is great for those with a sweet tooth - this recipe makes two, so curl up together and enjoy

- 400g vanilla ice cream
- 100ml Taste the Difference Irish cream liqueur
- 100ml full-fat milk
- 50g plain chocolate, grated, to garnish

1 Place the ice cream, Irish cream liqueur and milk in a food processor or blender, and whizz until combined.

2 Pour into 2 highball glasses and garnish with a sprinkling of grated chocolate.

Did you know...

The Dom Pedro is hugely popular in South Africa, where it is often served as a dessert

Chocolate dream

Calling chocolate lovers everywhere! This cocktail is the perfect indulgent treat and great for sharing with friends

- 60g dark chocolate, chopped, plus a little extra, grated, to serve
- 250ml full-fat milk
- 100ml Taste the Difference Irish cream liqueur
- 50ml vodka
- ice cubes

1 Place the chocolate and milk in a pan. Warm over a low heat, without stirring, until the chocolate has melted, then stir until smooth.

2 Remove from the heat, then add the Irish cream liqueur and allow to cool.

3 Stir in the vodka and some ice cubes, then strain into 6 chilled cocktail glasses and garnish with the grated chocolate.

Festive flavour

Liquid lemon meringue pie

The crushed meringue on these shot glasses gives a gorgeous frosty look, but its sweetness also balances the sharpness of the lemon

- juice of 1 lemon
- 1 meringue, crushed, to garnish
- 100ml basics vodka
- 2 tablespoons lemon curd
- 2 tablespoons single cream
- ice cubes

1 Dip the rims of 4 shot glasses in a little lemon juice, then in the meringue so the rims are coated.

2 Add the vodka, lemon curd, remaining lemon juice, cream and some ice to a cocktail shaker, then shake hard.

3 Strain into the decorated glasses.

Index